Facts About the Nuthatch

By Lisa Strattin

© 2016 Lisa Strattin

Facts for Kids Picture Books by Lisa Strattin

Saiga Antelope, Vol 104

Mudskipper, Vol 105

Vervet Monkey, Vol 106

Leopard Frog, Vol 107

Catahoula Leopard Dog, Vol 108

Musk Ox, Vol 109

Frigate Bird, Vol 110

Margay, Vol 111

Mexican Wolf, Vol 112

Indian Mongoose, Vol 113

Sign Up for New Release Emails Here

http://lisastrattin.com/subscribe-here

Join the KidCrafts Monthly Program Here

http://kidcraftsbylisa.com

All rights reserved. No part of this book may be reproduced by any means whatsoever without the written permission from the author, except brief portions quoted for purpose of review.

All information in this book has been carefully researched and checked for factual accuracy. However, the author and publisher makes no warranty, express or implied, that the information contained herein is appropriate for every individual, situation or purpose and assume no responsibility for errors or omissions. The reader assumes the risk and full responsibility for all actions, and the author will not be held responsible for any loss or damage, whether consequential, incidental, special or otherwise, that may result from the information presented in this book.

I have relied on my own observations as well as many different sources for this book and I have done my best to check facts and give credit where it is due. In the event that any material is used without proper permission, please contact me so that the oversight can be corrected.

Table of Contents

INTRODUCTION 6
CHARACTERISTICS 8
APPEARANCE 12
LIFE STAGES 14
LIFE SPAN 16
SIZE 18
HABITAT 20
DIET 22
FRIENDS AND ENEMIES 24
SUITABILITY AS PETS 28
BUILD A NUTHATCH BIRDHOUSE 39
KIDCRAFTS MONTHLY SUBSCRIPTION PROGRAM 40

INTRODUCTION

Nuthatches are small birds that live throughout North America. They live in a wide range of habitats. They have long beaks and white breasts. They will pair and mate for life. The female nuthatch builds the nests and incubates the eggs.

Nuthatches are very good at climbing up and down trees. They are also excellent fliers. They place nuts in the cracks of trees and eat a variety of foods. Nuthatches have a lot of enemies.

Nuthatches help control insect populations. They even eat some species of insects that people consider pests. They are protected by the United States Migratory Bird Treaty Act and are not able to be kept as pets.

CHARACTERISTICS

Nuthatches are very good at climbing up and down trees. They do this to store and find food. They creep up and down trees by clinging to the tree bark with their feet while searching for food.

Nuthatches get their name because they place large seeds and nuts in tree crevices and then pry them open with their beaks. They also store seeds and nuts in the cracks, crevices and loose bark on trees.

Nuthatches do not migrate, but stay and defend territories all year. Males will defend these territories, but both sexes live together within the territory. They will leave their territories in winter when food becomes scarce and join flocks with titmice and chickadees at bird feeders.

Nuthatches communicate with other nuthatches using calls. They are unusual in that they do not call a lot during summer or in their breeding season. They make the most calls during winter and early spring. Most of their calls are used for territorial defense and to warn other nuthatches to stay away. They also have very good eyesight.

APPEARANCE

Nuthatches are small birds. They have large head and beak. Their beaks are dark in color and turned slightly up. They have almost no neck and they have a very short tail.

Nuthatches are grey-blue on their backs with a whit face and stomach. They have brown rusty feathers on their legs and butts. They have black eyes. They have dark feathers on the top of their head and neck. This makes them look like they are wearing hoods. Their wings are black, gray, and blue in color.

LIFE STAGES

Nuthatches have three live stages. The first life stage is the egg. This stage begins when the female lays three to ten eggs in a nest made by the female. The average number of eggs is seven. The female will incubate these eggs for 12 to 14 days before they hatch and the juvenile life stage begins. The male will bring food to the female while she is incubating eggs. The juvenile stay in the nest for 26 days before they can fly. Once they can fly, they juveniles will stay with their parents for several weeks and learn to live and eat on their own. Then the juveniles will live on their own until they become adults. Both males and females reach the adult life stage around one year after birth. The adult life stage is the final life stage.

LIFE SPAN

There is no information about how long captive nuthatches live. In the wild nuthatches live an average of two years. The oldest recorded nuthatch lived 12 years and nine months.

SIZE

Nuthatches are small birds. They are four to six inches long and weigh less than 1/16 of a pound (less than one ounce). Their wingspans are 6 to 8 inches long.

HABITAT

Nuthatches live in deciduous (trees with leaves) forest, mixed forest, and coniferous forest (pine trees). They prefer to live in older mature forests. They like to have oak trees where they live. In the winter they will commonly visit backyard bird feeders.

They live in a wide range of habitats and are spread across North America from Canada to Mexico. They are able to take advantage of human development and can be found in parks, cemeteries, urban gardens, and orchards. They prefer the presence of mature or decaying trees in their habitat. These locations are ideal habitats for their preferred food. They are also likely to have oak trees, beech trees, and hickory trees where they like to find holes to build their nests.

DIET

Nuthatches are omnivorous and will eat almost anything. They use their excellent climbing abilities to move up and down trees looking for insects hidden in the crevices of tree bark, holes, and cracks. They also eat seeds and nuts. They will store seeds and nuts in cracks and crevices of trees to eat later. They get their name from placing seeds and nuts in cracks of trees and then ripping them open with their beaks. For seeds they prefer to eat oak acorns, beech nuts, and hickory nuts.

FRIENDS AND ENEMIES

Nuthatches are very social birds and have many friends. They are friends with other nuthatches. In particular, they pair and mate for life and live with their mate throughout the year. They will use calls to alert other birds to the presence of their enemies. Nuthatches are also friend with other birds like titmice and chickadees. In the winter they will join large mixed flocks of these birds. They will often be seen feeding together at backyard bird feeders. People are also friends of nuthatches. People place seeds and other feed in bird feeders in the winter. This provides a valuable food source for nuthatches to survive the winter.

Nuthatches are very small birds and have a lot of enemies. Hawks (sharp-shinned and Cooper's) are enemies of nuthatches. These birds will attack all life stages of nuthatches. Woodpeckers, squirrels, and snakes will attack adult nuthatches on the nest and eat the egg stage. Raccoons, domestic cats, and foxes will also attack adult nuthatches and are important enemies of this bird.

SUITABILITY AS PETS

Although they are non-migratory, they are protected by the United States Migratory Bird Treaty Act. This act makes it illegal to have them as pets. It also makes it illegal to have feathers, eggs, or nests from these birds. This makes nuthatches not suitable as pets.

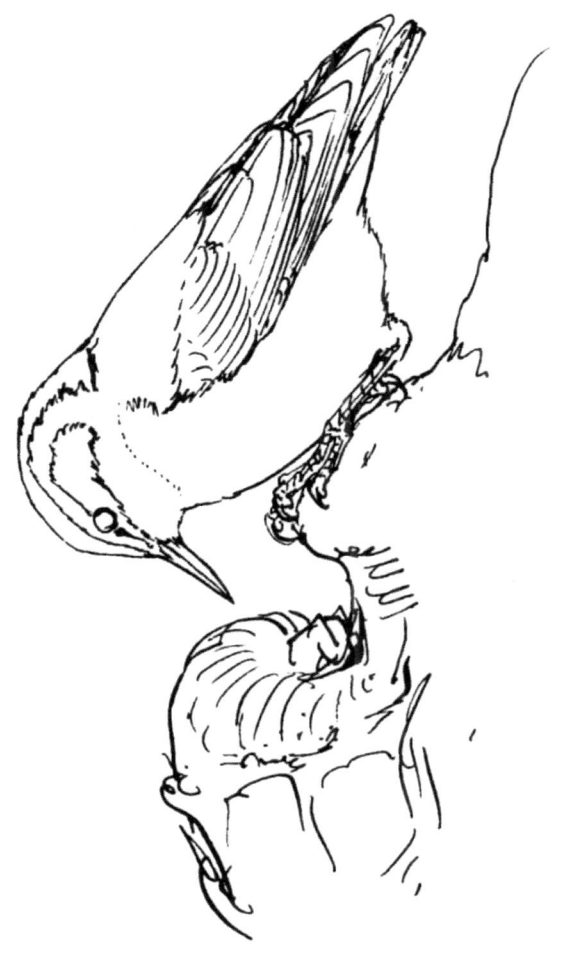

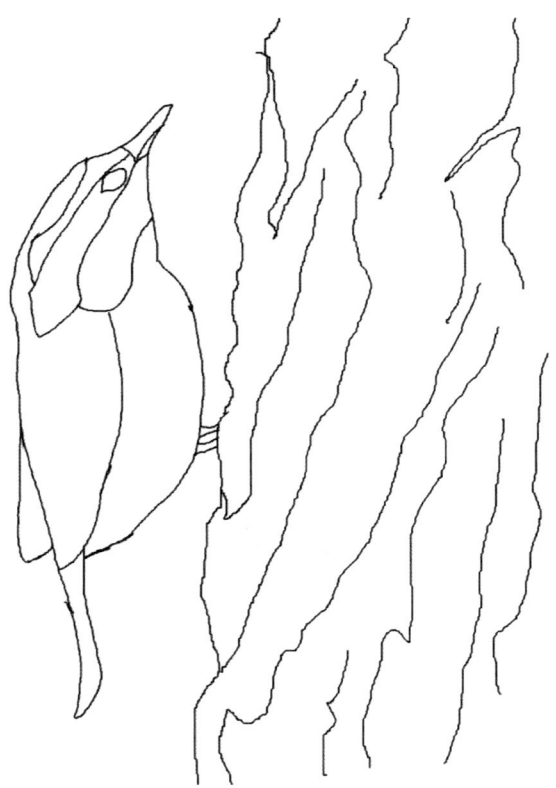

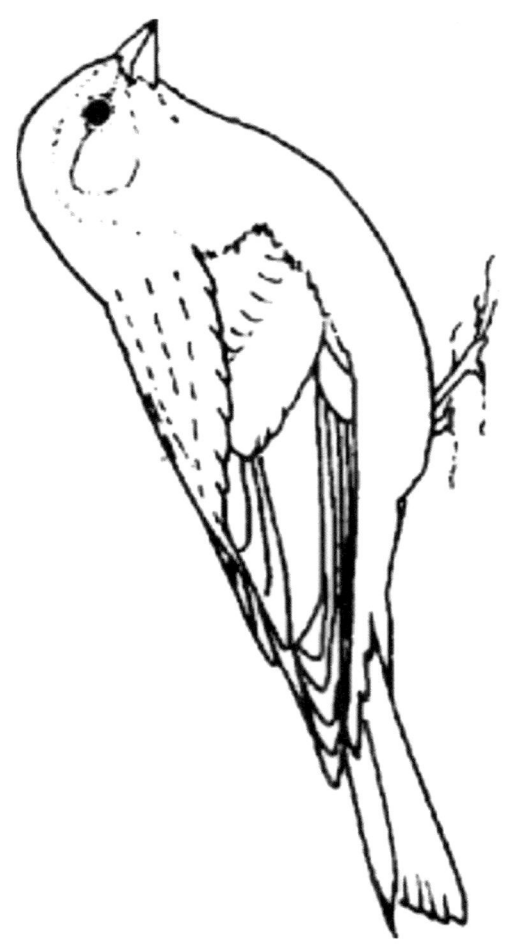

Please leave a review for me here:

http://lisastrattin.com/Review-Vol-122

For more Kindle Downloads Visit Lisa Strattin Author Page on Amazon Author Central

http://amazon.com/author/lisastrattin

To see upcoming titles, visit my website at LisaStrattin.com – all books available on kindle!

http://lisastrattin.com

BUILD A NUTHATCH BIRDHOUSE

You can get one by copying and pasting this link into your browser:
http://lisastrattin.com/nuthatchhouse

KIDCRAFTS MONTHLY SUBSCRIPTION PROGRAM

Receive a Box of Crafts and a Lisa Strattin Full Color Paperback Book Each Month in Your Mailbox!

Get yours by copying and pasting this link into your browser

http://kidcraftsbylisa.com

Printed in Great Britain
by Amazon